PREFACE.

THE purpose of the writer is to present a hand-book which shall make clear the mechanical procedures which the student of Kreutzer, if he would study Kreutzer properly, is obliged to consider; to put in black and white what every teacher discusses and shows in the lesson-room; and to so fasten these principles on paper that, unlike the spoken word, they may not go in at one ear and out at the other, necessitating tedious and costly repetitions, but may be referred to in the privacy of the study-room, as confirmations of what the teacher himself has said and done, refreshing the recollection, and fixing their facts on the memory.

It is often the case that in the long struggle through which the learner passes, technique is acquired unconsciously. The fingers, apparently, grow deft over night; and the amount of skill possessed is not realized until by some chance an account of stock is taken. This fact teachers have frequently noticed; they have, indeed, seen that even the listless playing of a study will benefit the student, regardless of his inattention and apathy. To the fitness of the technical material this is probably due — a fitness that brings about its result, anyhow, though not necessarily in the best and most satisfactory way. But, if good may be gained from a playing of these studies that is mechanical and perfunctory, how much more good may be drawn from efforts that are at all times conscious, and that are carried on with a definite and inspiring end in view, namely: the acquirement of the foundation technique needed in solo, quartet, and orchestral playing? And the possession of this is the result of a proper study of Kreutzer.

For to play Kreutzer well, with mastery of the bowings and fingerings laid down by Kreutzer himself — to say nothing of those laid down by many subsequent revisers — means three things:

First : On all four strings, a very considerable left-hand technique, comprising skill in shifting both up and down by seconds, by thirds, and by skips, an even strong trill, good double stopping in the four lower shifts, readiness in little finger extensions, smooth and rapid cadenza playing, and some skill in octaves, in diminished seventh chords, and in arpeggios — all of these executed by fingers held at all times quietly over the finger-board ;

Second : A bow arm, flexible, light, and yet firm and strong, well-trained and habituated in all the principal bowings, and ever ready, without stiffness in crossing the strings, to play these studies with an independent stroke in which neither bow arm nor finger hand knoweth what the other doeth ;

Third : A full even tone in all the registers of the violin.

In preparing this work it has been the writer's aim to describe as explicitly as he was able the various mechanical applications of the hands and fingers involved in playing these studies. If it would seem that the first studies had received undue attention, it must be remembered that it is in these very studies that the hardest work is done. For the last part of Kreutzer rarely gives any trouble.

The arrangement, the numbering, here followed, is that of the revision made by the author * and based on the revision of Edmund Singer, which contains, not the customary 40, but 42, studies. In closing, the author would acknowledge gratefully the aid he has found in consulting Carl Hering's *Ueber Rudolph Kreutzer's Etueden*, Leipzig, 1858, and the edition of studies revised by Emil Kross, Mayence, 1884, and in a little work of surpassing excellence, *l'Art de travailler les Etudes de Kreutzer* (The Art of Working-out the Etudes of Kreutzer), Lambert–Joseph Massart, Paris, 1897, the successful solution of some of whose problems may be attempted, however, only by the virtuoso.

B. C.

Boston, *Aug. 8, 1902.*

* For the Violin, FORTY-TWO STUDIES OF RODOLPHE KREUTZER. Edition based on the Revision of Edmund Singer, with Additional Bow Variants by Emil Kross and Lambert—Joseph Massart. Edited by BENJAMIN CUTTER, Boston, Oliver Ditson Company.

HOW TO STUDY KREUTZER

A HANDBOOK FOR THE
DAILY USE OF VIOLIN TEACHERS
AND VIOLIN STUDENTS

CONTAINING EXPLANATIONS OF THE LEFT HAND DIFFICULTIES
AND OF THEIR SOLUTION, AND DIRECTIONS AS TO
THE SYSTEMATIC ACQUIREMENT OF THE
VARIOUS BOWINGS, BOTH FIRM
AND BOUNDING

BY

BENJAMIN CUTTER

BOSTON
OLIVER DITSON COMPANY
NEW YORK
C. H. DITSON & CO.

CHICAGO
LYON & HEALY

ISBN: 978-0-359-08927-7

HOW TO STUDY KREUTZER.

GENERAL PRINCIPLES AND REMARKS.

The FINGERS. The finger last used in a shift is the one by which a change of shift is made; this act is done for the sake of precision; we call the finger involved the Shifting Finger, and the finger first used in a new shift, up or down, the Playing Finger. Sometimes one finger may act as both the shifting and the playing finger. We lay down, then, the following, —

RULE: *Unless the shifting finger be also the playing finger, the shifting finger must take its place in the new shift before the playing finger.*

The act of shifting may thus require one or two fingers.

Furthermore: Shifts may be made over the interval of a third, up or down, as in all ordinary scale playing — the so-called Scale Shift — moving over the shifts 1, 3, 5, 7, 9, or 2, 4, 6, 8; or, shifts may be made up or down a second, using shifts 1, 2, 3, 4, — Second Shifts — or, directly, by leap, to parts of the finger board more or less remote — Skip Shifts — 1 to 5, 6 to 1; these last may be called Guided Skip Shifts if a shifting finger be used, and Free Skip Shifts if no shifting finger be used.

The Bow. The four strings of the violin, when played singly, represent four planes through which the bow must pass; in double string playing, three intermediate planes are used according to the strings played upon. Freedom and uniformity of stroke demand that the bones of the fore-arm maintain the same relative position, one to the other, on all four strings and in whatsoever plane the bow may travel. For instance, to play on the G string with the elbow held down in the E string position, means to cross the two bones of the fore-arm unduly, and to exchange a position in which the muscles have all the freedom possible for one in which the wrist movements are cramped and the power of pressure is perceptibly lessened. Hence the following, —

RULE : *Raise or lower the upper arm from the shoulder at a change of string, so that the whole arm may be in the plane of the string or strings played upon.*

An exception in the case of a single short note on a neighboring string will often occur ; at such a time only the bow hand changes its position, involving a movement of the wrist.

Bowings divide, regardless of slurrings, into two great classes, the firm bowings, and the bouncing or bounding bowings. In either class wrist action is ever present, predominating, however, in the bounding bowings. The Fundamental Bowings, described in Study No. 2, will set this fully before the student.

STUDY No. 1.

A Minor — $\frac{4}{4}$ — Adagio Sostenuto.

Original Edition, No. 1 ; Massart, (omitted) ; Kross, No. 25 ; Schroeder, No. 5.

This study belongs well along in the set — before and preparatory to No. 23, the cadenza study — for it is in no way a proper No. 1. Its purpose is to give a legato, the famous long singing-bow of the classical school of violin playing, and the elements of this stroke may not be studied with the best success at this point in any ordinary violin course. The two essentials in the stroke are, pressure upon the string through the bow, and a fitting slowness in the stroke itself. The former element will be understood and will be easy after the Fundamental Bowings — see Study No. 2 — have been considered and practiced thoroughly ; and the latter element depends on a tension in the upper arm which counteracts the pulling or pushing of the bow, up or down. Exactly how much of these two elements is needed, must be told by personal observation alone. It should be remembered, at all times, that the finger pressure on the strings must exceed that of the bow. Still the student must not be over zealous in this respect, for a serious stiffening of the fingers is apt to follow attempts at too much tone through this means. The tone may be the safe side of a scratch. Economize the stroke at the beginning, whether the movement be up or down ; and do not despair of getting beyond the thin and puny sound which beginners always produce ; for, although little volume may be possible in the slurs over three and four meas-ures, still the benefit of the effort in playing them will soon show itself in increased purity and power, and in heightened command in all ordinary singing passages. It is advisable, after some skill has been gained, to use a swell and a diminish in each stroke, and a swell in one stroke and a diminish in the next. Finally : observe the Rule as to the shifting finger.

To increase the usefulness of this hand-book the numbering of the studies as shown by the following standard revisions has been given : David, Edition Senff ; Hermann, Edition Peters ; Blumen-stengel, Litolff ; Massart, Leduc ; Kross, Schott ; Schroeder, Kistner. Of these the first three follow absolutely in numerical succession and in number of studies the original " Forty Studies " by Kreutzer, and, with the countless reprints of the Forty Studies, are summed up under the head of Original ; the other revisions mentioned con-tain either forty or forty-two studies, with certain differences in their numerical order, of which a discussion is hardly necessary. As already mentioned, our numbering is that of Forty-two Studies.

STUDY No. 2.

C major — $\frac{4}{4}$ — Allegro moderato.

Original, No. 2 ; Massart, No. 1 ; Kross, No. 1 ; Schroeder, No. 3.

FINGERS. Although in C major and containing few acci-
dentals, this study is difficult of intonation. Scholars often play
sharp as they cross the finger board downward — a fact it is
well to know before beginning practice. With the measures
beginning :

keep the fingers together over the strings. Furthermore, shift
with the whole hand; do not push the first finger up or down,
and after finding the new shift move the hand with the other
fingers to fit this first finger. It is a fundamental principle in
shifting, that any finger must be in place to play in tune the
instant the shift is made, and if the fingers lag behind the shifting finger this cannot be done; the places of the fingers must
accordingly be taken as a secondary act in the procedure.

Bow. From the large number and great variety of bowings
invented for this exercise by different revisers, it would appear
that if studied long enough and properly, this study of itself
may serve as the medium in acquiring a very respectable and
comprehensive bow technique. Experience confirms this amply.
And for this reason we devote to this really remarkable exercise
an attention out of proportion to its apparent value. But the
skill which may be drawn from these five and twenty measures
may not be had at once. For, except in those rare cases in
which no trouble is met with at this point as to the intonation,
it is well to divide the attention at first between the fingers and

the Fundamental Bowings, and to discontinue and resume these bowings several times until their habits are confirmed, and their performance has become habitual, is automatic. For experience has shown that if, before his fingers have habituated themselves to playing in tune, the beginner in Kreutzer launches out into a variety of bowings, from distraction of his attention he will play false for a long time, and for a long time will suffer from the harm received just here.

A few words as to the philosophy of practicing, and the wisdom of the oft-repeated injunction, *practice slowly*, are here of importance. Man is a creature of habits. A wise provision of his Creator has caused all his acts to originate in so-called nerve impulses of two kinds that play into and aid the one the other. Any act done for the first time is done through a more or less intense effort of the will, through a volitional nerve impulse. Any repeated act, however, soon becomes automatic, a habit; is the affair of automatic nerve impulses. The volitional, or new, act means more or less nerve wear and tear, while the habitual act means a minimum of wear and tear. Herein is shown the wise provision of the Creator. For many of the complicated acts man is called on to perform, if performed often through the motor nerves alone, would soon reduce him to distraction, to physical ruin.

In the formation of the habit, **in the making of right and correct impressions on the sensitive and tenacious brain cells,** lies the point we would here emphasize. The quickness with which an act becomes automatic, in other words a *habit*, varies with different individuals, and also with the intensity of the willed act in the beginning. The slowness with which an act that has become automatic, that has become a habit, is changed for a better or other habit, closely or somewhat resembling it, is a matter of common knowledge, — a thing far beyond dispute or discussion. It is a matter always attended with difficulty; and the fact that teachers, the world over, in changing the position of the hand, for instance, insist on slow and attentive practice, well prolonged, goes to prove the weight of our words.

Let the Student ponder this. A word to the wise should be sufficient.

To serve our purpose, our peculiar purpose, we divide the various strokes of the bow arbitrarily into Five Fundamental Bowings. From these all the manifold modifications which

show the master player may be developed. To avoid any misun-
derstanding, it is necessary to say right here that there is no sign
save the printed word which shows absolutely which kind of
stroke shall be used in a given passage. This, quite like the
matter of touch in piano playing, is the affair of taste alone.

First Fundamental Bowing. The Forearm Bowing, the
détaché trainé of the French masters, the foundation stroke
used in all ordinary passage playing. Imagine the bow divided
into three equal parts, and draw the bow in the point third, at
each down stroke reaching the point itself. Speed is of no consideration; purity and volume of tone should be the aim. Fix
the mind on the beginning and end of each stroke, and see that
at these points there be no diminution in the amount of tone
produced, and no break during the change of tones, and no
slackening of the pressure on the stick.* Adjusting the whole
arm to each string by a proper raising or lowering of the upper
arm, draw the bow along so vigorously from the elbow that the
string, swinging sidewise, emits a full, clear, and even tone, the
opposite of that scratch tone due to an excess of pressure and
a lack of movement, or of that gauzy or whistling tone which
comes when the hair does not bite. Studied properly, improvement in quality and volume of tone will soon become apparent.
Play measures nine to fourteen, especially,

giving attention to crossing the strings without any breaks.
Hardly anything in Kreutzer will repay one better than assiduous

* As to pressure — It should be remembered that this is not made by bearing down with
the right arm and hand. Quite the contrary. Through the thumb as a fulcrum, a leverage
toward the left is made upon the stick by the fingers, hand, and forearm, — a steady twist
of the bowhand and forearm toward that point on the string where the force is expended,
where the hair of the bow rests. We believe that we are right in asserting that little or no
tone is made by the upper arm, except in chord playing, and, possibly, in that stiff-arm
slurred staccato for which Wieniawski was so famous.

and attentive practice of this bold and vigorous bowing. It must be made a habit. Once confirmed as such, the performance of the many slurrings which use it as their basis is comparatively easy. As a leading factor in all brilliant passage playing, — orchestral, quartet, or solo, — the student should not underestimate its importance, nor relax his efforts toward greater and ever greater mastery.

Second Fundamental Bowing. The quick Whole-Arm Stroke, the grande détaché of the French. Play each note with full bow at the utmost speed of stroke, pausing long enough between the strokes to fix the mind on carrying both arm and bow properly, on holding the bow still during the pauses, and on producing a clean-cut and full tone. Each stroke should begin with an attack, so-called. To do this the bow must grip the string to such an extent that full vibration begins with the starting of each stroke. This attack must be made at each end of the bow, and should be audible — a sharp, peculiarly biting, sound. Let the student apply so much pressure in the first place that, without moving the bow arm, he may shake his violin through this pressure on the string — holding the violin loosely meanwhile with chin and hand — and let him then relax the pressure enough to allow the string to vibrate under the starting of the stroke; his judgment will soon tell him how much pressure to employ. Rigid attention will soon make the attack, this indispensable point of technique, a habit, and will lessen very appreciably the matter of learning certain other strokes. This grande détaché bowing may also be played without an attack, the bow starting in the air before the hair strikes or touches the string — a form of stroke which is infrequent, the attack being commonly regarded as an indispensable element.

It is often noticed that about the middle of the stroke the bow swerves, or the wrist becomes stiff. This, in many cases, may be laid to an exaggerated bending of the wrist. For, although opinions vary as to the holding of the wrist — just how high or low — still the best players do not hump the wrist to breaking at the butt nor depress it to a letter V at the point. Begin the strokes, then, at the point third, if there be trouble, and lengthen them gradually until the middle of the stick has been passed, starting always with the forearm and the top of the hand in a straight line; which is the normal position, be it said. Lengthen the strokes until each end of the bow be reached, the wrist bending somewhat in the demands of the positions at the ends.

The element of tension should not be forgotten. Without proper tension a quick, clean start cannot be made. An excess is, however, harmful. The movement should be quick, free, and sure; and practice will make the arm light, ready, and tough, adding, like the First Fundamental Bowing, much to its endurance. Persevere until the habit of this stroke be formed.

Third Fundamental Bowing. The Hand Bowing.

Begin at the butt, short strokes, movement from the wrist alone. If the wrist be stiff — which, is often the case — the arm should be held against the door frame, or any immovable upright, until the bones of the wrist yield and the movement may be made without any participation of the arm. Go slowly until a fairly ample stroke is possible with fairly firm fingers — a very little play of the bow in the hand is not bad, although no play is better; the stroke may use one and a half inch of hair. Make it as sustained as possible, the tone effect a legato, not a staccato. The tone will not be loud. This peculiar stroke, with the effort to make a constant legato, loosens the bones of the wrist. When these are loose, repeat the stroke farther along the stick until it is easy anywhere. But, in doing all this, the forearm must be immovable, the whole arm acting only in changing the string.

Although regarded by many students as difficult, and by many never acquired — to their great loss — this stroke, on which so many things in good violin playing depend, may soon be played with ease and surety in a slow tempo. However, trouble is sometimes had in certain parts of the bow; in which case even the most perverse wrist, one most unyielding, may be loosened by beginning at the butt where the stroke is easy; then, the movement once started, the player may gradually work along the stick, making the up strokes shorter than the down, until the place be reached where the wrist is tight, taking pains the while to maintain the same relative position of the parts of the arm. Bear in mind that the action here is a lateral one, and that by laying the forearm and hand flat on a table and with still forearm moving the hand from side to side, the genuine motion may be produced. In actual playing, the axis of the wrist must be parallel to the stick of the bow, if one would make the pure motion; this means that with most hands the forefinger touches the bow, not on its second, but on its first crease, that the big knuckle be not low but high, and that the angle formed by the forefinger and the stick be near to a right angle.

In changing strings with this bowing, the pure lateral movement is modified, which is easy to understand. Where the changes are constant — A string, E string, A string, E string for instance — the hand, viewed from the front, describes a figure approximating an ellipse, the hair clinging to the string. Subsequent studies will offer ample opportunity to develop this peculiar and valuable feature of technique.

It is never wise to attempt to play this stroke fast in the beginning; better some time and quite a number of studies with it in slow tempo. Wait until the wrist has become flexible and enduring, and ready to respond to any change of string. Play each note four times, then three times, then two times, and at last singly, as written.

Driven at a fast rate with lightened pressure and shortened stroke, and at about one third of the bow length from the butt, the bow bounces naturally and gives the well-known **Spiccato** bowing, the French **Sautillé**, the **Bouncing** or **Springing** bow, so called. In this, both hand and bow play a part, that of the hand being the more important, since a skillful player with a poor bow can produce this stroke even half way between the middle and the point, where the bow will not bound easily and naturally unless used in a flying staccato stroke with the arm, the so-called staccato volant.

This springing bow, this spiccato, as usually taught, always requires a long time for its mastery, and is often never mastered at all; indeed its possessor is wont to be regarded with envy by the unclever and unsuccessful. The writer can see no just reason for this. This spiccato stroke, of which we speak, comes, in a natural way, from the hand stroke — and the hand stroke is readily learned. It is no use for the student to try to " catch the trick." There is no trick to catch. Let him learn the Third Fundamental Bowing; let him tarry with it, making changes of string with a closely clinging pressure, until the wrist moves automatically; let him persevere — and one fine day he will find that he has the two strokes. ▪But let him not underestimate the high value of the pure hand bowing, that without the bounce. If he will observe first-rate players, he will see soft and rapid non-staccato passages thrown off by the hand alone, and with a lightness and an ease not permitted by the forearm stroke; he will also see, as he studies on, how great a rôle this hand stroke plays in all the complicated slurrings the revisers of Kreutzer have employed — and he will probably be willing to master it as one of the indispensables.

Fourth Fundamental Bowing. The Saltato, the sautillé modéré, the thrown stroke, half arm, half hand, or, in certain cases, wholly hand.

> Not to be mistaken for the *sautillé*, the spiccato bow, although in France the two terms, saltato and spiccato, seem to bear the same general name, *sautillé*; not to be mistaken, we say, for the spiccato is a hand stroke and one of, if not the most rapid, of all bowings, while the saltato is not only limited in speed, but may combine both hand and arm, and differs also in the touch on the string.

With the wrist made free and supple by the hand bowing — and this is a necessity — play the whole study with up strokes, hand alone, at about the middle of the bow, or better, an inch or so toward the butt, lifting the bow from the string for the down stroke, arm still; repeat with silent up strokes, sounding down strokes, arm still. These are thrown strokes, blows on the string, and may be awkward and a little wild at first, and, because of the short touch of hair on the string, are always dry and somewhat cutting in tone. They should be as long as the side play of the wrist will allow. When mastered singly, combine up and down, without the silent strokes. Do not hesitate at the whipping of the string, or at the poor tone; these are at first unavoidable. While learning this factor, the following arm stroke, which is also a factor in the complete stroke, may be studied:— with bow in the middle and elbow brought forward to allow of free play of forearm and wrist, make light legato strokes, up and down, say two or three inches in extent, holding the hair on the string. When the forearm travels easily and the wrist is free, raise the bow from the string after each stroke, producing a sustained rather than a staccato effect, and shortening a little the former length of stroke. It will now be easy to shorten the strokes still more and to make them more or less staccato at will, both hand and bow now participating in the act which, though first made by the hand alone, has now become the union of the two elements, the Saltato Bowing itself. An expert will play this bowing with considerable rapidity; by the preponderance of the hand stroke or the arm stroke, it may be made very staccato or almost a legato. The beginner must not expect, however, too much speed; this is wholly a matter of growth; he should strive for lightness of touch and for absolute freedom of arm, upper and lower.

It is well to say at this point, that these bowings are used without any indicative sign. As already mentioned, the judgment, the taste, of the player is called upon. Thus:

devoid of marks of any kind, may be played with the hand bowing at any rate of speed from Adagio to Presto, or with the saltato stroke from a reasonably slow rate up to a moderate Allegro, but as a spiccato stroke only best and most easily at a rapid or very rapid rate. Modifications by • • • or ֍ ֍ ֍ may mean either saltato or spiccato; and – – – may mean the pure hand stroke, or a clinging saltato.

Fifth Fundamental Bowing. The Hand Staccato, the basis of the slurred staccato and of the martelé strokes. The first requisite is the Third Fundamental Bowing, the hand stroke; the other requisite is that grip of the hair on the string which we have called the Attack. With these two elements at his command, the student may combine them at any point of the bow and may produce a firm clean-cut tone, which will be the shorter and the more clean cut, that is the more staccato, the shorter the stroke with the hand and the more firm the grip on the string. It must, however, be a hand movement, not one of the arm. Amplitude of stroke rather than speed should at first be striven for, toughening and stretching the wrist. At the extreme point of the bow this stroke should be studied especially, until the wrist is strong and enduring, and at the same time, loose. It will take but little of this bowing to tire the beginner's arm, and it will take also but a few weeks' practice, usually, to improve the arm surprisingly, and to fit it for an easy mastery of the much prized and valuable Slurred Staccato, both up and down. The whole thing rests on the movement from the wrist, with a sufficiency of pressure — and, take notice, a sufficiency of endurance! From this stroke may now be learned, quickly, two, three, four, or more, notes in slurred staccato in all parts of the bow and up or down; and, from it, by lifting the bow from the string when it has become easy to make two or more firmly articulated strokes in the same direction, may be gained the bouncing or bounding Slurred Staccato, near the middle of the bow; and, later on, the Ricochet and Arpeggio strokes, all of which depend for their foundation not on the unaided spring of the stick, as is often supposed, but on the spring of the stick governed by the movements from the wrist. It is, however, advisable not to attempt too much at first in developing these many and alluring possibilities, however easy they may seem. They will all come, one by one, after the Fundamental Bowings have been learned — and this of itself is a matter of some time and effort. Furthermore, and to resume, by combining this hand staccato with a forearm stroke, the **Martelé**, the **Hammered Stroke,** so called, or what we prefer to call the **Forearm Staccato,** is easy to acquire, and should be practised with diligence; for of all bowings used in vigorous playing this is one of the most useful and general, and one of the most characteristic. It may be said here that this last stroke rarely receives the development it deserves, possibly because of the exertion it requires; in its place is employed a modification of the saltato stroke near the butt, whose effect is much different and which is used because it is easy.

With this stock in trade at his command, the student will now find many rough places made smooth. It will take time to learn all these bowings, and other studies, which busy the fingers, should be worked at, and pieces of various characters may be played with profit. Whether or not it is advisable to play all the bowings various revisers have fastened to this celebrated study, is an open question. The author has never known any one who has undertaken it with success, and has never ventured to require it; and in preparing his own edition,[1] he limited himself to those strokes which come into the general experience of players of all kinds. It will be noticed that he has laid stress on the Fundamental Bowings. Massart, however, whose eminent success as a pedagogue was shown by such pupils as Wieniawski, Sarasate, Sauret, etc., in his masterly little work, before mentioned, goes into great detail, and gives one hundred and fifty bowings and variants: legato, whole bow, grande détaché, forearm bow, sautillé, martelé, and then one hundred and thirteen varieties of slurring which depend on the forearm stroke; there

[1] See p. iv.

follow twenty-nine varieties of slurs and of slurred staccato, employing the bow in different parts, and finally two versions in octaves.   This may do well for the Paris Conservatoire, where a subsidy from the government places the school in a position to dictate any course of study, however severe.   But it does not seem adapted to the wants and conditions of this country.   In actual playing, and in the course of an extended experience, perhaps a fourth of this number may be called for.   We do not, then, consider the study of all these bowings necessary.   Provided one has acquired a certain amount of skill, many of them are only a matter of reading.

Finally, as to Working-Up-to-Time, acquiring speed: — It is our impression, confirmed by experience, that time and effort are wasted in attempts to play fast, because the powers of attention and of observation are dissipated by the playing of too many consecutive measures ; dissipated to such an extent that the relationship of the tones is not caught as they pass by the ear. Just herein lies the greatest difficulty of the violin — the tempering of the tones, the adjusting of their relationships.   This is often shown when a pianist of experience and schooling, his ear and his judgment apparently established and settled, takes up the violin.   Students of this class have been known to do as badly as the boy who plays his first scale on the violin.   The trouble lies in the adjustment of pitch.   Cut the exercise into groups of nine notes, as in Example No. 1, or into a variant of the nine note group in which the bow takes up its motion before the fingers begin, as in Example No. 2.

The brevity of such a group allows close attention in a slow tempo to the pitch of each tone, and to the adjustment, the tempering, of all the tones ; after which the group may be accelerated until a high rate of speed is gained.   But the powers of criticism may not be allowed to flag. After several groups have been treated in this way and each goes in tune, put two, then three, together at the increased rate of speed, starting the bow beforehand on the reiterated note and straining the attention keenly as to the pitch. Follow this out; go through the whole study in the same way; begin to play habitually in tune in a fast tempo.

STUDY No. 3.

C major — $\frac{4}{4}$ — Allegro moderato.

Original, No. 3.; Massart, No. 2; Kross, No. 5; Schroeder, No. 4.

FINGERS. A sequence exercise, containing three different figures.* The first figure, one of four notes, falling by seconds through twelve repetitions, is easy. In measure 4 begins a rising eight note figure, moving by seconds and quitting the first shift in measure 10. The Rule: Unless the shifting finger be also the playing finger, the shifting finger takes its place in the new shift before the playing finger — finds application here in measure 10, and from this point on. The shifting finger, 2, which plays the two lined g,† must move to a'' before the playing finger, 4, seizes its own note, c'''. This act is repeated until the descending figure is reached, the hand in shifting upward measuring the distance taken by the touch of the shifting finger on the string, and by the drawing away of the hand from the finger tips and around the corner of the violin. An excellent means of learning this necessary and fundamental procedure, is as follows:

---

* A sequence is the transposition, more or less regular, of any group of notes. Such a group of notes is called a *motive* or *figure*.

† For the sake of accuracy, the total scale has been divided into octaves, so-called. Each octave begins with a C. The lowest tones of the violin belong to the small octave, g, a, b; then follow the one lined octave, c' to b', and, in natural consequence, the two, three, and four lined octaves — c'' to b'', etc.

the shift note being used as an appoggiatura. When mastered, omit the appoggiatura.

Two things must also be emphasized here. In shifting no higher than the fourth shift it is customary to keep the thumb about opposite the first or second finger; but, if the shift be higher, then the thumb should be drawn back in season to allow the hand to swing naturally and easily around the corner of the violin, and, by causing the four large knuckles, the roots of the fingers, to assume a line as nearly parallel as possible with an imaginary line drawn down the centre of the finger board, to make it easy to place the fourth finger cleanly and accurately on the A string. Furthermore, it is necessary to preserve the volume of tone as one climbs up the finger board, and this can best be done when the position just mentioned is assumed; for only this position seems to allow the finger tips to maintain an undiminished pressure on the strings when the fingers themselves from being bent sharply, become extended and lose their sharp angles.

In the falling sequence, the four note figure presents less difficulty. Hold the first finger firm in shifting. In measures 13, 14, 15, instead of using the first shift and the open string, preserve the sequence by taking the fourth shift.

It is often beneficial to play the rising and falling shift notes by themselves with the shifting fingers; thus:

This seems to impress the measurements, the spacings, on the sense and to make their performance more sure. In closing we would lay stress on the fact that this study is about as important for the fingers as was its predecessor for the bow. Master it.

Bow. Anything done in No. 2 may be done here, but it should be remembered that as this is essentially a finger study and the finger difficulties are considerably greater than those of the bow, the bow requirements should be moderate.

STUDY No. 4.

C major — $\frac{4}{4}$ — (no time sign given).

Original, No. 4 ; Massart, No. 3 ; Kross, No. 3 ; Schroeder, No. 2.

Aside from one or two extensions, the fingers have almost nothing to do. The bow has the work. This study is generally begun too soon and without proper preparation, which we may attribute to a desire to learn this special bowing, a desire inherent in all violin players; for the stroke is justly prized as an ornament of great value. But studied too soon, it has cost many and many long hours of unavailing toil. If, however, the Fifth Fundamental Bowing, with all that goes with it, has been mastered, the way is clear, and one may attack this stroke without loss of time. For at the bottom of the whole thing lies a simple mechanical procedure, and although special aptitude when possessed does help, still the power to articulate staccato notes strongly and clearly from the wrist, is the main thing. Hence the importance of the bowing just mentioned. Furthermore, under favorable circumstances (we would emphasize the word, favorable), the student will have played and learned a dozen other studies and a number of pieces before mastering the staccato stroke.

Those who find the up staccato stroke difficult, often find the down easy; which they may learn by first playing with the stick turned toward the face, then held straight over the string, then in the normal position, turned away from the face. Use all parts of the bow, until the middle and point are as free from difficulty as the butt. Then reverse things, and try the up stroke. The forearm must be held back, in other words, restrained, as much as possible; indeed, an excellent exercise is that of playing with an immovable forearm while the bow is carried back by the hand after each up stroke; the slight sound that the recoil makes disappears in the real stroke, and the gain in many cases is a great one. Very often a hand, naturally stubborn, is by this means taught the whole trick in a short time — provided the hand staccato, the Fifth Fundamental Bowing, has been well practiced.

The long accented note at the end of each slur should be played scrupulously in time, and with plenty of bow; likewise, the accented first note in each measure.

STUDY No. 5.

E flat major — $\frac{4}{4}$ — Allegro moderato.

Original, No 5; Massart, No. 4; Kross, No. 2; Schroeder, No. 1.

FINGERS. When played perseveringly, without the open strings — measures 6, 11, 13, 19, 21, contain exceptions — the fingers soon become stretched out over the finger board in a natural and excellent position. Aside from a drill in flats, this seems to be the point of the study. Drive to a rapid tempo — eventually.

BOW. A great variety of strokes is both possible and valuable. We would recommend as special strokes, Nos. 5, 9, 10, 12, 17, 18, 19, 20, of our revised edition (Oliver Ditson Company).

5.   9.

Nos. 5, 10, and 12 may be played with the flying staccato, the staccato volant, the bow being used at about its middle and leaving the string partly by means of the hand stroke, a derivation of the saltato; these, with the firm or hand staccato, will be the better bowings to first practice. Too great stress cannot be laid on Nos. 17 and 18, which should be taken up after Study No. 6 has been mastered.

STUDY No. 6.

C major — 4/4 — Moderato.

Original, No. 6 ; Massart, No. 5 ; Kross, No. 6 ; Schroeder, No. 7.

In measure 17 begins a sequence, passing through the shifts 1, 3, 4 :

Meas. 17.

In measure 19 beginners are apt to reach too far for the
highest note, forgetting that it is only a minor second above the
high E, and in measure 20 the shift of only a major second —
e″ down to *d″* — is often exaggerated by a half tone.

Very helpful in playing the three octave scales is a clear
mental picture of the tones on the E string stopped by the first
finger.   Namely: measure 23, the thirds *b″, d‴, f‴*; measure 25,
c‴, e‴, g‴; measure 27, *d‴, f‴, a‴*.   These are the successive
members, root, third, and fifth, of three triads (a triad is a three
tone chord) formed on three rising and consecutive scale steps.
They may be played very profitably, alone, with the shifting
fingers, as was done with a passage in Study No. 3.

In measure 29:

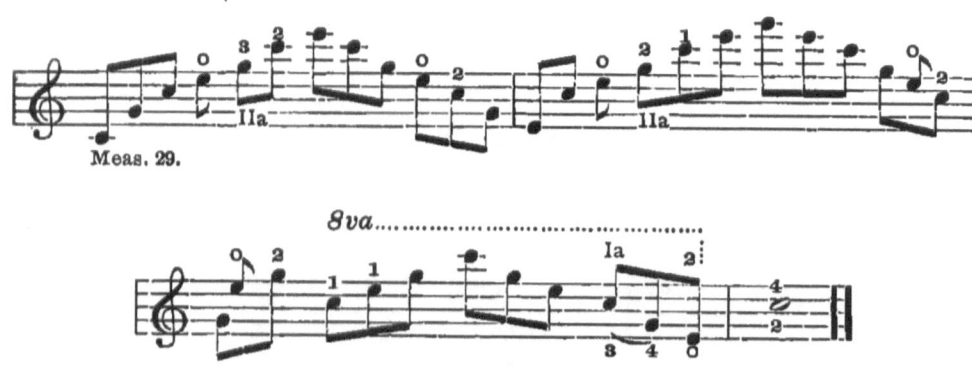

a free skip shift is made while the open E is played.   Hold elbow
well under the violin.   Learn to place the hand in position without stopping the strings — without touching them with the
fingers.   The outside fingers, 1 and 4, should be in place for
the octave *e″, e‴*, the thumb falling vertically against the butt
of the neck in taking the shift, and the first finger being about
opposite the thumb, thus acting as a guide to the hand.   It

should be remembered that as a general thing the position of the thumb in the four lower shifts remaius the same, provided that the hand goes no higher, and that in all shifts to the fourth position the touch of the thumb is a sure help, if the violin be rightly built.

It may be said, however, in this connection, that the place of the thumb is not fixed and inalterable. Some excellent players hold it invariably behind the fingers, so bent back from the large knuckle that it serves as the only support of the neck: the hand thus approaches the neck when the lower strings are used, the thumb projecting considerably beyond the G string side of the neck itself. In using the E string, the opposite thing obtains: the hand quits the neck, goes to the right, and the thumb is drawn laterally under the neck until its tip, or comparatively little, is seen on the G string side. We do not advocate this holding, nor do we censure it; but we consider it worthy mention, especially as we have seen it employed by violinists of recognized standing and of the best schooling. Furthermore, it is said, on good authority, to be the position used by Paganini, the position which made easy his indescribable flourishes on the G string.

Measure 30 — In taking the skip to the fifth position, while the arm swings to the right, the thumb falls back behind the first finger and following the hand as it, the hand, moves both upward and outward, the thumb passes along the G string side of the neck just around the swell, until the butt of the neck itself is reached, which the thumb strikes between its tip and its first joint; at this point in the act, with the hand well around the corner of the violin, the fingers should be found over their places, ready for use. This procedure, somewhat complicated, demands that the violin be held firmly by the chin and shoulder.

Bow. This is known as a martelé study. Lay stress on the up stroke, that it may be equal in vigor to the down stroke. The higher the note, the longer the stroke, to compensate for the greater thinness of string. Massart gives a number of useful bowings, the best being:

STUDY No. 7.

D major — $\frac{4}{4}$ — Allegro assai.

Original, No. 7 ; Massart, No. 6 ; Kross, No. 7 ; Schroeder, No. 6.

FINGERS. This study has been regarded as a bow study, prin-cipally ; but its value for the fingers is almost as great as that of any of the Kreutzer studies. The fingers should be held down as much as possible ; which stretches them over the finger board and gives them a good shape — a matter not all done at once, but which once done will well repay the student for all his pains. The fourth finger extensions in measures 35, 36, 37, 38, will need special care.

Bow. As a martelé study this is one of the finest in exis-tence. It is customary to play the high notes with an up bow, the low notes with a down. Profit may be had if this be reversed. Draw bow to extreme point ; place it cleanly on the string before starting the stroke. The upper arm should be fairly immovable, perhaps not altogether so ; and must assume, if we may so express ourselves, the position — as the case may be — for the plane of an imaginary or actual intermediate string. The upper arm should also control by a proper amount of tension the amplitude of the stroke, which must become the shorter the higher the rate of speed. Use a bold and sharp stroke; with neat beginning and ending. Also, a vigorous, a very vigorous, hand throughout. For vigor of right hand and forearm enters into all brilliant playing. To gain this, slow practice and the keenest watching of the tone are required. Massart recommends as the first bowing, the *grand détaché*, then the *martelé*, and lastly the *saltato*.

STUDY No. 8.

E major — $\frac{6}{8}$ — Allegro non troppo.

Original, No. 8; Massart, No. 7; Kross, No. 8; Schroeder, No. 10.

FINGERS. Like Studies 5 and 7, this one brings the hand out over the finger board. It has its difficulties — the sharp key, and some extensions and contractions of the fourth finger. But the main thing is to first get the intonation correct; then one may drive the tempo, all the time keeping the fingers where they belong. When mastered, a marked improvement in the shaping and the readiness of the right hand will be apparent. Mastery means, however, a pretty good rate of speed, and as a general thing this study is, in this respect, never half learned; it is given up too soon, and its real good is never enjoyed by the pupil.

BOW. Practised at the extreme point of the bow, a fair speed means the acquirement of a light and ready running bowing, of great value. The slurrings are useful, but most useful in general playing is this light running stroke at the point. In crossing the strings the hand must move freely from the wrist.

If practiced enough, this stroke will become exceedingly neat and clean ; nimble, indeed ; a great ornament in one's playing. The spiccato is recommended by Massart, also different forms of staccato ; of these, to our mind, the staccato volant is the most useful, and in the following form :

The part played by the right hand in this bowing must not be overlooked. It is not a stroke depending in the first degree on the elasticity of the stick, and in the second degree on the function of the hand — but just the reverse. For, as in the case of the spiccato, an adept will perform it finely with a miserable bow, devoid of elasticity. The firmly articulated slurred staccato is necessary at first — in playing which the wrist must cause the hair to cling to the string ; when the wrist performs its functions, regardless of the changes of string, the staccato volant will not prove difficult.

STUDY No. 9.

F major — $\frac{3}{4}$ — Allegro moderato.

Original, No. 9 ; Massart, No. 8 ; Kross, No. 4 ; Schroeder, No. 9.

FINGERS. Although preparatory to the trill studies and in a sense the first of them, it is evident from the results of its practice that this study was written with more than one purpose in view ; the frequent changes in the place of the half tone, often at each alternation of stroke, make it an intonation study of the highest order. The element of first importance, then, is the spacing of the fingers. To fix this in the mind, the whole piece may be played profitably without the bow, simply by placing the fingers for each figure simultaneously on the string. Thus: measures 1, 3, 5, 7, 9, 10, will give this:

six shifts, in taking which shifts the first finger, which does most of the work, must be firm and sure.

It has also been found useful, in order to further emphasize this important detail of shifting, to play simply the first note of each shift with its proper finger. Thus:

Practiced faithfully, these preparatory exercises save time. For, the intonation in the many shifts being assured, the attention may be given undividedly to relaxing the hand and to gaining in the shortest time that speed, flexibility, and endurance which are some of the aims of this study.

Persevere until the fingers go. There are places where the hand will cramp, or where it does not seem to fit the strings easily. Take these slowly and with a relaxed hand, and remember that this study, with all the good stored up in it, may not be learned in a short time, and that the fingers will not feel all the good right away.

Furthermore, gratifying success has attended the use of two other methods. The one is to play the study without the bow, striking the fingers audibly on the finger board, but avoiding any cramp; the other is to play the study with the bow, as written, and to hold down the unused finger in each slur on a neighboring string. Of the former method much may be made; of the latter, a little will suffice.

Bow. Aside from the prescribed slur, the spiccato and the

saltato are excellent, notably the former stroke ; also that light,
running bow at the point, recommended for the preceding study,
and a slurred variant of two down and ten up bow notes, staccato on the up bow, at will.

STUDY No. 10.

G major — $\frac{4}{4}$ — Moderato.

Original, No. 10 ; Massart, No. 9 ; Kross, No. 9 ; Schroeder, No. 11.

FINGERS.   Measure 4 :  Fifth shift

taken by skip from the first shift ; or from the third shift,
this third shift being taken as a go-between, a poor procedure
but one that is at times recommended to awkward pupils. ·In
either case the first finger takes $f\sharp''$ on the A string, before or
with the fourth finger, the octave, $f\sharp''$ $f\sharp'''$, being thus seized by
the octave fingers, 1 and 4.   To reach for the highest tone with
the fourth finger, and to then draw the rest of the hand after this
finger, is uncertain and hence wrong ; the hand should go into a
position with any finger ready to take its own tone naturally and
in tune.   Furthermore, as the preceding figure fits the octave, d'
d'', so this figure fits its own octave, $f\sharp''$ $f\sharp'''$, and viewed in one
light all the free shifts in the study are shifts to octaves.   Consequently as much care must be given to the first as to the fourth
finger, the first finger taking its place by a free skip, or moving
along the string as a guided shift from some lower position.

Measure 13:

Sixth shift taken. Two methods: guided skip shift — the first finger moving from *d''* to *g''* along the A string; or, free skip shift — the hand moving upward without the guidance of any finger until the hand and fingers are over the proper place. The first method is the better one to begin with. If, now, the elbow be brought well around and the knuckles are in proper line with the finger board, it will not be difficult to finger this whole passage, some two or more measures, in the sixth position, the first finger clinging to the string and crossing the finger board on the tones *d'''*, *g''*, *c''*, *f'*, the fingers 3 and 4 falling as cleanly and firmly on the G string as on any other string; this depends, however, on getting the elbow round to the right, and on holding the hand sufficiently high. Hold down the fingers !

Measure 17:

Skip to fifth shift. The first finger may pass up the A string to *f'''*, this shift being taken freely by skip, or one may place the first finger on *f''* on the E string, and use a guided skip shift to *c'''*, when it will be easy to place the fourth finger in tune. We prefer the free skip shift, the first procedure, in which the first and fourth fingers go to the octave, *f'' f'''*.

The special good of this study lies in the broken chord, and in the free shift. Only after the fingers are at home is it wise to take any but the plainest bowings. Massart gives a few versions, the most useful being a slurred staccato of the 16th note groups, which may be played with a firm or a flying stroke.

STUDY No. 11.

E major — $\frac{4}{4}$ — Andante.

Original, No. 11 ; Massart, No. 10 ; Kross, No. 11 ; Schroeder, No. 6.

The object here is not only to get a good legato, but to shift
without altering the relative holding of the fingers one to
another ; in other words : to shift with the hand and not with the
fingers.   One frequently sees a hand which has played the first
triplet in tune, move to the third shift with the fingers 2 and 3
huddled closely together or crowded against the fourth finger.
This is wrong.   For, to play in tune, after gaining the new shift,
the fingers if held thus must be first drawn back to their proper
places before they may be used; which means unnecessary
motion ; and in the mechanics of the best violin playing, as may
be observed, unnecessary motion is excluded quite as rigidly as
in a first class machine or engine.   To obviate this fault, employ
the Rule as to the shifting finger until the fingers have become
independent and set ; thus :

Care must be taken of the thumb, which, as the rudder of
the hand, stays behind the fingers and moves about freely.   Hold
violin tightly by the chin.   The hand must be free.

STUDY No. 12.

A minor — $\frac{4}{4}$ — Allegro moderato.

Original, No. 12 ; Massart (omitted) ; Kross, No. 13 ; Schroeder, No. 12.

If any study in Kreutzer requires slow practice for a long time until the fingers become set and infallible, this is the one. It is a common thing to find scholars who play the first six or ten measures in tune and at an average speed ; later in the study they become self-conscious and timid, weak in tone, they hurry, and play out of tune, and perhaps from their lack of success become fearful and tender of all high tones whenever met, unless these high tones come in scale order when the measurements are easy, and confidence is good.   This should not be.   It is generally the careful but bold player who plays in best tune in the high shifts. Hence, slowness, and a firm long bow and firm steady fingers, are earnestly commended.   If the ear be dull in measuring the extreme high tones, all the more reason for keen attention — for by concentration of mind any sense may be made more sharp and discerning.   The technical difficulty of getting around the corner must be considered, and the left elbow be held well under the violin.   Make each group the object of special consideration. One bowing is amply sufficient.

STUDY No. 13.

A major — $\frac{4}{4}$ — Moderato.

Original (not included in the " Forty Studies ") ; Massart, No. 11 ; Kross, No. 14 ;
Schroeder, No. 13.

We have here the first of the double stop studies. Let us emphasize this fact — **the first of the double stop studies.** And let us say, further, that if instead of playing the book straight through in its numerical order, Studies 1 to 42, as is usually done, the pupil, after finishing this study, takes up slowly and by bits the much dreaded last ten studies, following the directions given in No. 32, he will save much time, and will be the gainer in the end, and will have the satisfaction of feeling that these studies are little, if any more difficult, than many others in the set.

FINGERS. Reduce the figures to their lowest terms, to the bare chords, thus :

and play the study through as a pure chord study. Hold down the fingers. Except where a shift is made, one finger should help the other in finding its place. Thus, in measure 3, finger 4 is guided and made sure of intonation by the touch on finger 3, held down on the next string. In those measures where the figure does not require three strings, where it fits two strings, as in the fifth measure, the two upper tones of each figure may be played. But, if one would play in tune, the strings must be well gauged ; indeed to play on strings which are not properly sized, is to do one's self a positive harm. Finally, some exacting extensions occur. Hold down the fingers !

BOW. A great variety of strokes is given by Kross, and by Massart. After learning the original bowing, which requires a loose wrist with the bow at the point, the slurred and the staccato three string arpeggios may be practiced. Play the staccato arpeggio with the bow held on the string, hand staccato, until the wrist articulates ; then attempt the bounce, concentrating the stroke, so to speak, by avoiding a long bow, while accenting the first note in the up stroke until both hand and stick respond.

STUDY No. 14.

A major — $\frac{4}{4}$ — Moderato.

Original, No. 13; Massart, No. 12; Kross, No. 12; Schroeder, No. 14.

FINGERS. An intonation study of the first order, which, after the fingers begin to go, may serve to develop the bow. Hold the fingers close to the strings throughout.

Measures 9, 10, and 11:

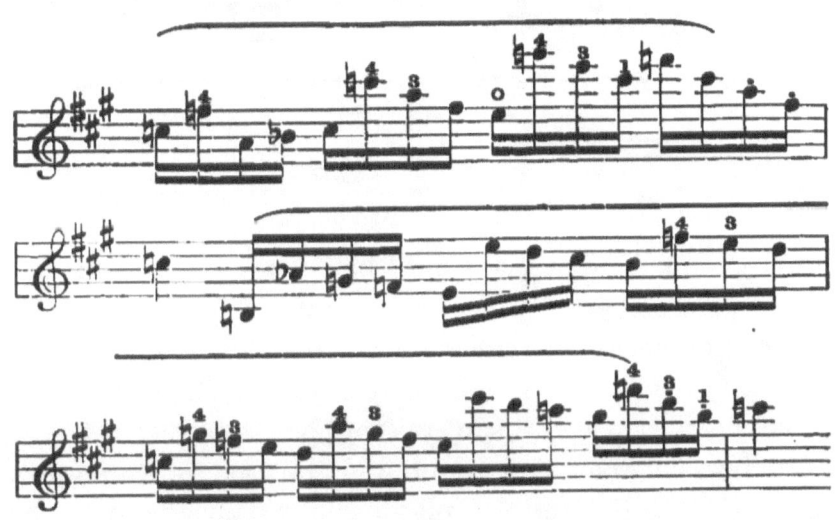

In measure 9, three extensions occur; two from the first shift (easy) and one from the fifth shift (difficult), the hand in this latter case swinging around the corner, finger 1 falling over the tone *c'''*, the finger 4 being at the same time extended for the high note *g'''*. In measures 10, 11, the changes of shift are made by sliding the first finger over the tones *c''* and *d''* to *e''*. The fourth finger must not reach out into the new shift and draw the hand after it; the whole hand must move, the shifting finger taking its tone first of all. This technical procedure we have already discussed; but the frequency with which one meets with faulty shifting prompts us to again mention it.

Measure 25: The second finger shifts from *g″* in the fourth group to *c‴*, as the shifting finger.

Measures 40, 41:

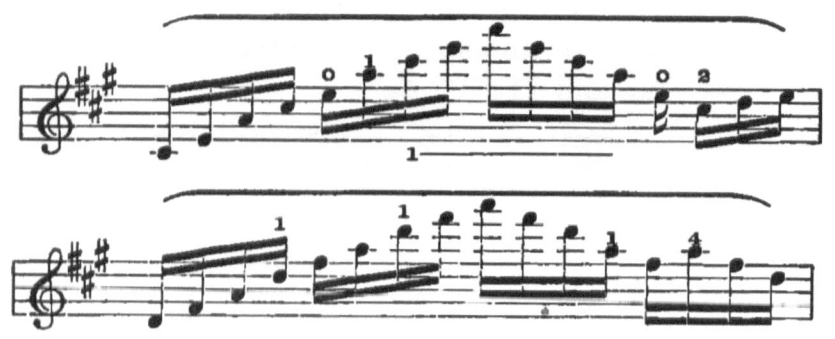

Swing the hand freely around the corner in shifting upward. Draw the thumb back before going into the third shift. We would mention again, in this connection, that many of the best violinists play with the thumb bent freely backward behind the hand, the neck of the violin resting on the thumb instead of being pinched between the thumb and the base of the forefinger. Such a holding facilitates the playing of a passage like this one in question; it allows the hand to move freely and with the least hinderance. Furthermore, we would say that in extensions, except in those which follow the open string, some lower finger must be held down to keep the hand in place. This difficult study should be played until flexibility has been gained. So considerable are some of the difficulties that to master them means a decided growth of ear.

Bow. To perform the given bowing properly, amounts to possessing a good smooth tone, economy of stroke, and a lightness of wrist which fits the bow to the many changes of string. The saltato and spiccato strokes are recommended; also, and especially, that light running stroke at the point recommended in Study No. 8. Preparatory to the spiccato, play assiduously with the hand stroke, causing the hair to cling closely to the string, to search it out, as it were. This gives the wrist practice in that elliptical movement without which no one can play this spiccato stroke in this study. As a study for this especial bowing, this is one of the first in the literature, and the student will do well to appreciate its importance.

STUDY No. 15.

B flat major — $\frac{4}{4}$ — Allegro non troppo.

Original, No. 14; Massart, No. 13; Kross, No. 15; Schroeder, No. 15.

Special aim: to develop a third finger trill. Rapidity or closeness of beat is of no importance here, of no consequence for some time. The desideratum is a series of perfectly even beats, easily and freely made, an act in which the finger springs like a flash to do the command of the will. This may be gained only by slow practice; especially of the following variant:

So much endurance must be acquired that the fingers remain unjaded at the end of the study. Furthermore, do not grasp the string too firmly. Stiffness may result from this as from too much trilling. Quality of practice should be striven for, rather than a quantity of notes, and the student should never forget that a good trill is a matter of growth, and that all healthy growth takes its own time and cannot be forced.

There are measures where the hand will feel tight, awkward, constrained; practice these slowly with a loose hand until they go. We do not advise a short trill; at least eight notes in the trill and turn will repay best. We cannot see why this study and the following study should be played with short spasmodic trills, as is usually the case. One charm of the trill is that it may begin its warble insensibly, as it were, and not with an accent. We believe, also, that the accent hinders the finger action and that the too early study of the short trill is injurious, that it tends to give many hands a cramp; and we have found that when the finger has become free and ready, it will make a short trill with little study.

STUDY No. 16.

D major — $\frac{4}{4}$ — Moderato.

Original, No. 15 ; Massart, No. 14 ; Kross, No. 16 ; Schroeder, No. 16.

We have found that this study also yields the best return if practised slowly with quite a long trill; as follows:

This method does away with the harmful "cramp trill" of one or two beats; which may be learned very quickly and safely when the long trill is easy, and without any danger of stiffening the fingers. This method also gives beats enough to call for a sustained and even effort, which we have found to be unequalled in loosening and strengthening the fourth finger.

As in the preceding study there are places where the fingers go hard; not so much from weariness as from a certain awkwardness of position of the hand and fingers. Play such places separately with relaxed hand.

Massart gives the following excellent variant, which may be played spiccato, or legato with the hand stroke, unifying admirably the bow and the little finger.

STUDY No. 17.

B flat major — $\frac{4}{4}$ — Maestoso.

Original, No. 16 ; Massart, No. 16 ; Kross, No. 19 ; Schroeder, No. 17.

The union of a bold martelé stroke with an easy, clear, and brilliant trill figure, makes this an interesting and valuable study. If these two elements are known beforehand — and they should be, in the nature of things — the study may be learned quickly. Let the trills be equally fluent throughout. Play with vigorous hands and fingers. The trill figure may be further developed, thus:

STUDY No. 18.

G major — $\frac{4}{4}$ — Moderato.

Original, No. 17 ; Massart, No. 17 ; Kross, No. 20 ; Schroeder, No. 19.

Requires great endurance of finger, the trills on the G string tiring the hand very quickly. All trills in the shifts 3 and 4 on the two back strings, must be played slowly and with a loose hand until easy. As in the other trill studies, the learner will come across places where his hand will feel helpless, awkward; due to position of the hand, and, very probably in this study, to weariness of finger. Play slowly. We repeat a previous statement — a good trill is a matter of growth. Hence a little a day is much better than any strenuous effort to take the trill by storm and to thus learn it in a short time.

We take occasion here, to recommend what may to many seem a bold innovation, namely: **the beginning of the double-stop studies at this point in the course.** Their position in the original edition does not argue that the double-stop work must be taken up after the other work has been done. Nor does the fact that nearly every subsequent edition presents these ten studies as the end of Kreutzer defend satisfactorily this place at the end of the course. Experience has shown that, aside from the fact that these studies are no more difficult than many of the passages in single stopping, if these double-stop studies be begun now, they will act as a relief to the many trill studies, and the pupil will in the nature of things devote many more weeks to the consideration of two-string playing than is ordinarily the case, and, from the element of gradual growth thus fostered, will play them better than if taken at the end of the course — and in consequence will life-long be the gainer thereby. The very fact that they come at the end of months of study in Kreutzer, causes not a few scholars to slight what should be given plenty of time. If these studies were more difficult, or far more difficult, than those which preceded them, to our way of thinking there would be all the more reason for beginning them betimes.

But actual experiment has shown that they may be begun and studied with the greatest profit at this point in the course, and that they are less difficult than some single string passages.

To return — In measure 2, which is a sample measure, the trill is taken by a change of shift, and with the auxiliary (upper) and not the principal (lower) note. Take pains that in all such cases the hand reaches the shift before the finger is put on the string, and do not strain the finger in an effort to start a quick trill. These places should strengthen fingers 3 and 4, although as generally practised they often do harm. Clearness, evenness, and ease, come before speed; which is a matter of growth and should not be sought for too soon. A thorough review of No. 9 will do good here.

STUDY No. 19.

D major — $\frac{4}{4}$ — Moderato.

Original, No. 18; Massart, No. 15; Kross, No. 22; Schroeder, No. 18.

Plain in appearance, this study is very far from easy. The difficulty consists in shifting with the third finger, and in using, without cramping or stiffening either fingers 3 or 4, this same third finger as the principal finger in the trill. Those measures which use the second finger in shifting give so comparatively little trouble, that we do not consider them at all. Any attempt at speed will usually produce very quickly one or the other of the above faults — stiffness or cramp — and will defeat the object of the study, which is to develop a running third or fourth finger trill. The best means toward this end is the following variant:

The quiet carriage of the hand, and of the finger to its proper
place, must ever be borne in mind; it is absolutely necessary, is
the thing of first importance.   If the fingers are to work well
there must be no clutching, also no hurried change of shift.
Play the variant above given, first with the hand bowing,
patiently and slowly.   When it goes, the spiccato may be tried
and that light running stroke at the point mentioned so many
times.   After this, and lastly, the slur.   And when this variant
is easy, the other variants may be tried, the one beginning with
the auxiliary note of the trill being for many hands very awkward and troublesome, through the inclination to clutch the
string nervously in shifting — the very thing which should be
avoided.

This very excellent study is usually neglected.   Through its
neglect the hand is deprived of that permanent strength and of
that freedom which will surely come from study sufficiently prolonged and continuous.   To play it without slurs, unifies the
bow and the fingers remarkably, and to play it well in this
way means to possess both brilliancy and fluency of a very useful
kind.   If what one may learn from a study defines its character,
this neglected study is one of the very first in the entire set.

STUDY No. 20.

A major — $\frac{4}{4}$ — (no time sign).

Original, No. 19; Massart, No. 18; Kross, No. 24; Schroeder, No. 21.

Also one of the best studies in the book. Play it first without the trill, as a plain scale study ; for as such it is unrivalled and serves as a fine drill in taking free shifts and in crossing the finger board. Massart treats it, with various bowings, as a trill and as a scale study. Of these bowings a slurred staccato of the sixteenth notes, and the spiccato stroke, are the most useful. Also, if played without trills and with a vigorous forearm stroke in rapid tempo, this study will give, when mastered, boldness and clearness, especially if begun with an up bow; but the D and G strings must be made to yield their tone in these high shifts, even if one has to force them a little.

As to the shifting, we can say nothing better than that the fingers 1 and 4, the so-called octave fingers, must both take their places at each change of shift; in other words, the hand goes to the shift as if an octave were to be played. If, now, the outside fingers are in tune, the other measurements are easy. But — bring the elbow well around to the right that the back strings may be fingered with facility, and hold down the first finger as much as possible. When the scales go smoothly, add the trills. The fingers should work cleanly and vigorously ; and no matter what the position, they should not chafe against one another.

STUDY No. 21.

D major — $\frac{4}{4}$ — Moderato.

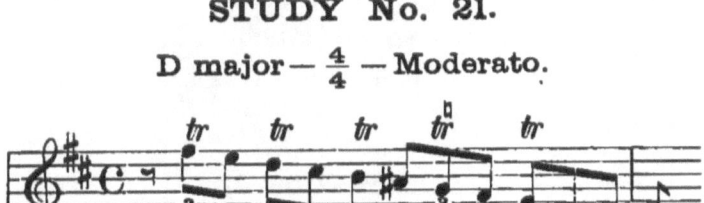

Original, No. 20 ; Massart, No. 19 ; Kross, No. 17 ; Schroeder, No. 20.

A companion to No. 19, in that fingers 3 and 4 are called on to do the shifting and trilling. If No. 19 is known, this study will be easy to play. Utilizing it in another way, and besides making this a good slurred staccato study by repeating each tone,

Massart gives some exceedingly valuable triplet variants, which aim at lightness and rapidity and represent a phase of technique that the violinist will find indispensable. We recommend these variants as more valuable than any trill practice.

spiccato.

STUDY No. 22.

A flat major — $\frac{4}{4}$ — Moderato.

Original, No. 21 ; Massart, No. 20 ; Kross, No. 23 ; Schroeder, No. 22.

We have never seen any special merit in this study and would not advise the student to spend much time on it. If the foregoing studies have been well learned, this one may be despatched very quickly.

STUDY No. 23.

B flat major — $\frac{4}{4}$ — Adagio.

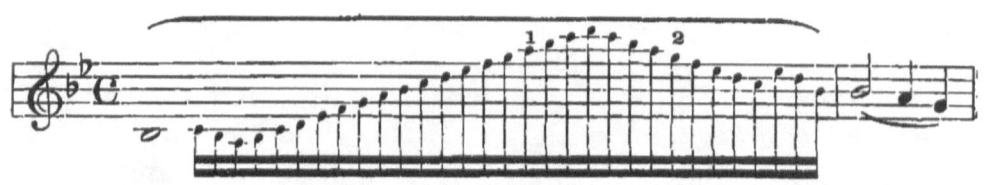

Original, No. 22 ; Massart, No. 21 ; Kross, No. 26 ; Schroeder, No. 23.

Most scholars, because they attempt too great a run at first and in so doing fail to hear what they are playing, go to pieces on this study, and waste both time and strength, and often at last regard its successful performance as problematical. But if, for instance, the first and second cadenzas be broken, as follows:

No. 1.

No. 2.

and be then put together, the results will be most satisfactory. For the different elements of these runs will then have been considered in detail, which experience has shown to be the quickest way to master them. Furthermore, although the general impression prevails that the cadenza is a run without time — which may in a sense be true — to the learner it is not a run without accents, although these accents may be hidden in the general sweep of the whole thing. In many of the runs the first note is tied; this tied note is the accented note, notwithstanding, and the note which follows it the unaccented note. The accentuation of the triplets is plain. In those measures in even notes which begin without a tie, accent the first note.

As to the bow; it is well to break the slurs until each run goes smoothly. Then play as written, and spare the bow at the beginning of each stroke. Furthermore, the study of a swell and a diminish in each slur will give skill. Indeed, this Study should be preceded, if one would extract all its goodness, by a careful consideration of Study No. 1; the scholar will then have a long bow at his command and may devote himself, without distraction, to his fingers.

STUDY No. 24.

G minor — $\frac{4}{4}$ — Allegro.

Original, No. 23 ; Massart, No. 23 ; Kross, No. 27 ; Schroeder, No. 24.

It has been found useful and time saving to play this study all through as a single finger study; as follows:

This means, to play all the upper notes with the proper fingers, as if octaves were being played, and then the lower notes in the same manner. After the thing goes well, put the fingers together and play the study as it stands. This method helps many hands to learn the measurements most quickly. But we would warn the enthusiastic student against any prolonged practice of this study; and warn him earnestly, too. For the fingers are easily made stiff, and a little practice at a time is the best and safest plan, is the only safe plan. The difficulty of this study is slight, and no extra bowing seems necessary or possible.

STUDY No. 25.

G major — $\frac{4}{4}$ — Allegro moderato.

Original (not included in the "Forty Studies") ; Massart, No. 22 ; Kross, No. 21 ; Schroeder, No. 25.

Study in the same way as No. 24. Difficulty, slight. The scholar who has learned the foregoing studies more than half way, must have unconsciously played octaves for some time; for the free shifts in Nos. 6, 10, 14, and 20, if played properly, are nothing more than octaves taken by the octave fingers, even if not sounded. So, let him take up and finish these two studies with the assurance of success. Bow variants are suggested here, and the saltato stroke is as good as any.

STUDY No. 26.

E flat major — $\frac{4}{4}$ — Moderato.

Original, No. 24 ; Massart, No. 24 ; Kross, No. 28 ; Schroeder, No. 26.

Skip shifts, scales, extensions, and fingers held down and out over the finger board, are the features of this study.   In crossing the finger board in high shifts, bring the elbow well around to the right, and place fingers 3 and 4 on the strings with especial care and strength, for these are the fingers which give most trouble in the higher positions.

Measure 20 :

Skip to fourth shift; let the thumb strike the butt of the neck, guiding the hand, after which the thumb may be drawn back to allow the change to the sixth shift in the next measure.

Some of the extensions are awkward, and are made more easy by bending the first finger backward and sideways from the large knuckle — or the tenths may be changed to octaves.

By persistent study learn to drive this at a rapid pace, and play with a bold and vigorous stroke.   Massart gives several bowings, of which we would suggest the grande détaché, the spiccato and the saltato, and the firm forearm stroke ; also, as or exceeding value, the running point stroke.

STUDY No. 27.

D minor — $\frac{4}{4}$ — Moderato.

Original, No. 25 ; Massart, No. 25 ; Kross, No. 18 ; Schroeder, No. 27.

An intonation study, pure and simple. Although Massart gives nine bowings, experience shows that all reasonable profit may be gained from the given slurring, with or without accent, from the light running point stroke, and from the whole measure slur. If the preceding studies have been well learned there is little in this study that will give any trouble, provided the tempo be moderate ; but to play it in good tune at a rate rapid enough to fit the spiccato stroke, for which Massart calls, requires a very ready and expert set of fingers — which are not often possessed at this point. The difficulty lies in the frequent contractions and extensions. These, as much as anything, characterize the study and demand a very quiet hand with unusual side play from the large knuckles of the first and fourth fingers.

STUDY No. 28.

E minor — $\frac{4}{4}$ — Grave.

Original, No. 26 ; Massart, No. 27 ; Kross, No. 29 ; Schroeder, No. 28.

Although this is a violin solo of a high order, and is not to be regarded as a purely technical study, yet it has always seemed to the writer that Kreutzer aimed, first of all, to furnish a study in the legato ; the long slurs with constant changes of string, the slurred leaps to high notes, the many extensions that must be made so neatly that they are unnoticeable, all going to prove this.

There are few things that require discussion; unless possibly the long rising leaps, in which the Rule as to the shifting finger loses its force, the hand travelling freely upward until, the position being found, the finger seizes the string. In all extensions the under finger must be held down firmly.

STUDY No. 29.

D major — $\frac{4}{4}$ — Moderato.

Original, No. 27 ; Massart, No. 26 ; Kross, No. 10 ; Schroeder, No. 29.

This study, the last of the single stop legato studies, has been given the tenth place in the Kross edition. And as the tenth study it may be played — but surely not with the hope of extracting all its goodness. Massart gives it the regular place, which we prefer, and cites twenty-nine modes of playing, the most difficult being a transposition an octave higher, which, with the like transpositions of other of these studies, is the affair of one with an established and considerable technique, who reconsiders these studies when a mature player. To apply some of the bowings is, however, highly profitable. On account of the constant change of string, the hand stroke may be studied with great benefit, and from it, when the wrist has become limber, strong, and quick, may be gained a clear spiccato. Patient persistence is necessary. The bounce on one string is easy; it is the constant change of string, to which the wrist must fit itself, that forms the difficulty, and the bow will not bite the string unless a supple wrist has first caused the hair, so to speak, to search out the string. The saltato and the light running forearm stroke are recommended.

But, as in No. 27, to play this study in a rapid tempo, requires a clever and very ready left hand. And to acquire this, means — work.

STUDY No. 30.

B flat major — $\frac{4}{4}$ — Moderato.

Original, No. 28 ; Massart, No. 28 ; Kross, No. 30 ; Schroeder, No. 30.

To be gained — a brilliant forearm stroke, some extensions, three- and four-string chords broken into arpeggio figures, wrist endurance, clearness of tone in the fourth position, and, last but not least, fulness of tone all across the violin. The bow should take firm hold of the string throughout; the thumb and fingers of the bow hand have this to care for, and not the elbow which often, in this study, goes into the air, tightens, and tries to share in the making of tone and in the change of string. Massart gives this study altogether without slurs ; this, if one would play clearly, certainly calls for a very clean, clinging, and biting stroke, and is far from easy — although beneficial to the arm. Keep at the point throughout. The broken chords may be played in two ways ; thus in measures 13, 14:

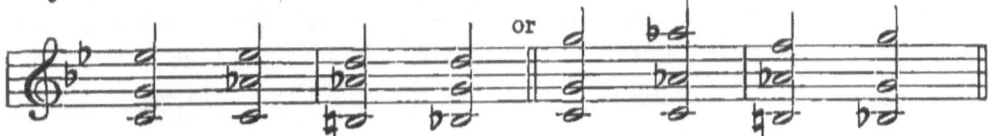

STUDY No. 31.

C minor — $\frac{4}{4}$ — Allegro.

Original, No. 29 ; Massart, No. 29 ; Kross, No. 31 ; Schroeder, No. 31.

The points here are : the half tone, a short, rapid trill, and a vigorous and especially tough and enduring forearm stroke. To play well in a slow tempo ought to give little trouble ; but to play it only fairly well at a rapid rate, means a great deal. For, if taken up to time, both the half tones and the trills are very difficult.

It may help the matter of intonation if the student knows that the chord structure, almost throughout, is very simple and apparent. Thus, this figure :

is the backbone of measure 1, each member of this C minor chord being preceded by its minor under second as a foreign tone — what some theorists call an appoggiatura. If the chord tones are known, the appoggiaturas, generally minor seconds throughout, not major, are easy to play. Hence it is advisable to go over the whole study several times, playing only these principal tones, the second tone in each two-note slur ; then, when these tones are in the fingers, it will be easier to learn the study in its entirety. Passages without these appoggiaturas may be omitted when found, as in measure 42, for instance :

Only diligent work will make the fingers quick and ready, even when the chords are known and the intonation is established.

STUDY No. 32.

F major — $\frac{4}{4}$ — Andante.

Original, No. 30; Massart, No. 30; Kross, No. 34; Schroeder, No. 32.

For the bow, a fine legato study; for the fingers, a master-piece in extensions, not to mention the double-string work. There is nothing new to say about shifting. But we may call attention to the part played by the fourth finger. From the very beginning this finger must go firmly and boldly to its place in the new shift, and the third finger must measure from the fourth finger its major or minor sixth; it is accordingly the fourth finger that takes the new position — not as is often done by scholars, the third finger, the under finger in the shift. The slur may be broken; indeed, the best way to study this at first is to use eight strokes in the measure. This allows one to get the fingers in shape before thinking of the study of a legato, which is a secondary element.

From this study should be gained increased volume and purity of tone, a tough, true, and ready fourth finger, and, if we may so express ourselves, an adaptability of the fingers to fit themselves to the strings, to the finger-board, which will make all the following double-stop studies, in a measure, easy. Still, we believe that this study should be preceded by No. 34; indeed, the preparatory exercise for two or more strings was No. 13, already discussed.

We must say again, and we would lay stress on our words, that these double-stop studies should not be put off until all the single-stop studies have been taken. No. 34 may follow, very nicely and naturally, No. 13; after which No. 32 may be taken with success; and if these double-stop studies are then carried on little by little, time will be saved, and the learner will not look forward to the end of Kreutzer with dread, a dread unfounded and useless, and often paralyzing in its effect. These last studies are easier than much that precedes them. We base this statement on the supposition that the student has been trained to hold his fingers properly over the finger board, and, in certain passages, down on the strings, which, be it said, is the only way to finger the violin, the non-observance of which is, perhaps, in greater part responsible for the trouble some students have here with double stopping. If this book is played through according to the numerical order of its exercises, a loss of time ensues that at the least may be called unfortunate, and that is needless and unpedagogical.

STUDY No. 33.

F major — $\frac{4}{4}$ — Andante.

Original, No. 31 ; Massart, No. 31 ; Kross, No. 35 ; Schroeder, No. 33.

A study essentially for thirds, with many extensions. The chromatic pushing up and drawing back of the fingers is also a feature. The bow has nothing to say. In measure 21 begins a sequence :

the third chord in each group is a fifth, sometimes a perfect fifth, requiring one finger; again an imperfect fifth, requiring two fingers. This is the interval by which the shift is made. Consequently it is the interval most needful of attention. Play this sequence — some six measures — with detached bows, before slurring.

Of this difficult study Massart gives four variants, all transpositions — an octave, a perfect fourth, a major sixth, and a major seventh, higher. We believe that the ordinary student will be satisfied to play the original as it stands, and we are sure that it is all that he should attempt.

STUDY No. 34.

D major — $\frac{4}{4}$ — Moderato.

Original, No. 32 ; Massart, No. 32 ; Kross, No. 32 ; Schroeder, No. 34.

The difficulty comes here at the chord changes, not in the middle of the figure. Play this first as a chord study, pure and simple.

When mastered in this way, the goodness of the study may be easily extracted, namely: double strings with expansions and contractions, strong and independent fingers, a good legato, and a flexible wrist, especially needed in seizing the back strings with the up-bow, and, last but not least, all-round endurance. For those places where the fingers go hard, patience, a relaxed hand, moderation, and persistence are highly recommended.

Massart gives a number of bowings and variants. It is striking that the first and second are the grand détaché and the sautillé; it is striking, too, that this great teacher, throughout his treatise on Kreutzer. lays so much emphasis on these two so radically different strokes — on the acquirement, first, of firmness of tone, and of accuracy of finger, and then on the acquirement of clearness and lightness.   To return — one will find useful here the saltato, and a spiccato variant of twice-repeated notes.

STUDY No. 35.

E flat major — $\frac{4}{4}$ —Allegro moderato.

Original, No. 33 ; Massart, No. 33 ; Kross, No. 33 ; Schroeder, No. 35.

There is little to explain, technically, in this piece.   What is required is seen at a first playing.   As has been done before, it may be well to reduce some passages to their lowest terms. Measures 17, 18, 19, 20, will give this triple stop figure :

STUDY No. 36.

E minor — $\frac{4}{4}$ — Allegretto.

Original, No. 34 ; Massart, No. 34 ; Kross, No. 36 ; Schroeder, No. 36.

We have here the same thing that we found in No. 32 — a change of position in which the fourth finger, by free skip, seizes the string, the third finger measuring from the fourth.   This is met at once in the first measures. There is nothing, otherwise, that will cause any trouble or extra work. Play at the extreme point, and also a little farther up the stick. The second of the slurred notes must receive the most bow.

STUDY No. 37.

F minor — $\frac{4}{4}$ — Allegro vivace.

Original, No. 35 ; Massart, No. 35 ; Kross, No. 37 ; Schroeder, No. 37.

As it is generally most easy for the beginner in double and triple stopping to grasp one tone after the other, it is quite possible that the main object of this study is to train the fingers in seizing three and four strings in high and low positions. The figures should be studied as chords, and the remarks on this point made in certain preceding studies will suffice here. A forcible, compressed stroke at the extreme end of the bow is recommended, strengthening and making flexible the forearm. The detached sixteenth notes may also be taken with the slurred staccato, up and down.

STUDY No. 38.

D major — $\frac{4}{4}$ — Moderato.

Original, No. 36 ; Massart, No. 36 ; Kross, No. 38 ; Schroeder, No. 38.

We have never known this excellent legato study to give any trouble. If played long enough, it strengthens the tone and

makes it smooth, and renders supple the fingers. It may be
used with fine results as a saltato study.

STUDY No. 39.

A major — $\frac{2}{4}$ — Allegretto.

Original, No. 37 ; Massart, No. 37 ; Kross, No. 39 ; Schroeder, No. 39.

Also a legato study, utilizing the first four positions. In
measure 40 begins a figure (Letter B, Edition Ditson):

of which frequent use is made, and containing an extension of
the fourth finger. Play these measures with a specially firm
hand. The diminished fifth plays an important part in this
study.

STUDY No. 40.

B flat major — $\frac{3}{4}$ — (no time sign.)

Original, No. 38 ; Massart, No. 38 ; Kross, No. 41 ; Schroeder, No. 40.

Although it does not contain a single double trill, this study
has been called one of the best double trill studies in existence.
At any rate, he who can play the whole study through with a

clear and enduring trill, and without becoming stiff, will probably
have little trouble with any double trill he may happen to meet.
In learning it, care must be taken not to play too much at a
time — quality, then, rather than quantity.

Played with the Massart trills :

and without the slurs, as a spiccato study, this piece will give
brilliancy and staying power, the bow problem being a considerable one.   In this form it may be regarded as a successor of Nos.
16, 18, and 21.

STUDY No. 41.

F major — $\frac{4}{4}$ — Adagio.

Original, No. 39 ; Massart, No. 39 ; Kross, No. 42; Schroeder, No. 41.

A legitimate and natural outcome of what has gone before.
To play it in tune and with a fair tone, should be easy ; to play
it with a fine, noble tone is the matter of much study — study
that will, however, show its reflection, its general effect, in all
sustained playing.

STUDY No. 42.

D minor — $\frac{4}{4}$ — Moderato.

Original, No. 40 ; Massart, No. 40 ; Kross, No. 40 ; Schroeder, No. 42.

No new element is introduced here. To play this excellent fugal piece clearly and vigorously, is not easy, although, like its predecessor, it follows naturally from what has gone before. It calls for a clean bow, and clear fingering, and is a worthy ending of this surpassingly useful set of studies.